Radical
Psychoanalysis

Radical Psychoanalysis

and anti-capitalist action

Ian Parker

Resistance Books

Ian Parker is a practising psychoanalyst in Manchester and a revolutionary Marxist. He also writes, and his books include *Socialisms: Revolutions Betrayed, Mislaid and Unmade* (2020: Resistance Books) and, with the Mexican revolutionary David Pavón-Cuéllar, *Psychoanalysis and Revolution: Critical Psychology for Liberation Movements* (2021: 1968 Press).

Politicians of all stripes now talk about 'mental health'. They tell us how they have suffered, and promise more resources to put things right. At the same time, welfare services are being cut, people are told to sort problems out for themselves, and the state is beefed up to deal with dissent. With increasing misery comes increasing anger, some of it directed at capitalism and some of it turned around against ourselves, even into ourselves, so this sick system also makes us sick. Energy that could overthrow this rotten system is turned around to sabotage our collective struggles for a world beyond capitalism. Mainstream 'mental health' and 'wellbeing' programmes are too-often focused on making us change our thoughts, urging us to be happy, and fit in. But there is an alternative. The alternative comes through political action, through anti-capitalist resistance and many other political struggles, and this is where radical psychoanalysis can be our ally. But to make it our ally we need to know what it is and what it could be. Another world is possible, and psychoanalysis opens up possibilities for personal and political change.

Radical Psychoanalysis and Anti-Capitalist Action

Ian Parker

Published 2022
Resistance Books, London
info@resistancebooks.org
www.resistancebooks.org

Cover design by Adam Di Chiara

ISBN: 978-0-902869-29-5 (print)
ISBN: 978-0-902869-28-8 (e-book)

CONTENTS

1 Why do we suffer?   1

2 What are we?   15

3 Where is psychoanalysis now?   27

4 What use is it?   41

5 What can we make of it?   61

FURTHER READING   69
WHAT IS A*CR   73

Why do we suffer?

Human beings suffer and also, against all odds, they thrive. They do both in very different ways in different cultures and at different points in history. We suffer now from a sick world, a capitalist world, and the suffering is quite specific. It takes different forms for each of us, and that is why a psychoanalytic approach to suffering listens to us one by one, listening to our distress, our different ways of living and barely surviving in this world.

We cannot pretend to understand completely the complicated and hidden ways each one of us suffers, but what we do know is that capitalism as a sick system is grinding us down while it destroys the world. Capitalism, a system of political-economic domination, also intensifies other forms of oppression, including sexism and racism, and it turns us from being the ones who can change the world into our own worst enemies, so we become attached to our misery while blaming others for it.

Separation and conflict

We want a world where we can live and work, be creative and happy, but we are torn apart and torn from each other, while those who benefit from this terrible destructive exploitation rub their hands and encourage us to join them. Those in positions of power and privilege want us to scramble upwards, treading on everyone else, as they do.

The false promise is that by working our way up, and abandoning those who suffer alongside us, we can be happy. The promise is that more money and more power, especially power over others, will relieve our misery. In the process this might, those in power hope, even dissolve our knowledge that things are wrong, that this kind of world is built on lies. Ideology that tells us we cannot change is a system of lies. It is just not true that we cannot change, be otherwise.

Separation and conflict in this sad world are quite specific to capitalism; this is *alienation*, which has awful effects, and which psychoanalysis has insights into, insights into the depth of suffering and into the way distress paralyses us and turns our energy for change into resentment at each other.

Alienation as competition

We are already separated from each other in the market-place for labour power. That labour power is what we sell in order to get a wage, what we must sell in order to survive. Labour power is not only physical but also mental, and mental labour in a software company for example, is then treated as superior to physical labour. It is not, but that feeling of superiority is part and parcel of the competitive world in which we sell our labour power, a world that alienates us from each other. We then compete to get the job, compete to keep the job, compete with foreigners, who, we are told, are threatening our jobs; and we resent those who seem to have cushy jobs.

In this way, alienation as competition with others drives us into our own little individual selves, the tiny world of the individual body separated from others, and we become convinced that it is only individual struggle and individual success that counts. This is ideology. This is the false self-destructive world, and the private inner world, where we imagine that all that counts is the 'I', what is good for 'me'; this self-contained individual 'me' is what psychoanalysis calls the 'ego'. Some psychoanalysts aim to strengthen the ego, to adapt it to society, to enable us merely to survive, help us compete, but radical psychoanalysis reminds us that there is more to us than this.

We are who we are with and alongside. Psychoanalysis describes how we patch together our sense of self, our 'ego', from our relationships with others. Early relationships are crucial, but this is a process that continues throughout life, something we notice in the way we borrow words and phrases and little tics from those who are close to us, as well as from the media.

But another world is possible, and also possible is another way of being human. Then we can come to be who we are among others, with us, tackling that competitive alienation in collective struggle.

Alienation from our bodies

Psychoanalysis shows us how this miserable separation from other people in the world of work under capitalism also separates us from our own bodies. Each of us locked into our selves must sell our labour power, and that labour power is there in the body that takes us to work or in the brain that must produce something for a wage. So, alongside the fear that someone else will take our job is the fear that our own body will break down, let us down, even turn against us.

Our bodily 'health' is then intimately linked to our 'mental health'. We become anxious and depressed about what our body cannot or will not do. And we have enough examples around us to learn that those with bodies that are not healthy enough will quickly be 'disabled', turned into the waste of this rotten system.

Alienation from our body then becomes something toxic, and we may live our distress through our bodies. We know friends and relatives who have already done this, been broken and stuck in misery in which their bodies seem to cry out for them to be heard.

Psychoanalysis listens to how our alienation and misery locks up what we want to cry out, locks up our distress in our body so that a physical symptom takes the place of that distress and speaks for it in disguise, or locks up our distress in the mind so that the thought that we have failed, or some other self-destructive thought, goes round and round inside our head.

Ideas and images of what a normal body is like, and what we are told is weak or 'abnormal', then feed these symptoms. Images of women as weak or irrational or even as 'hysterical' when they complain, or of gay sexuality as a sign that something has gone wrong, or of the black body as savage, uncivilised, then make it so that the individual symptoms also operate as social symptoms.

Then we live out different forms of oppression in our bodies, locked into them. The question, which radical psychoanalysis helps us answer, is how we might find space to speak and be heard and take action to change the conditions that lock us up inside ourselves.

Alienation from nature

That is not all. Capitalism as an economic system based on the drive for profit and the enrichment of a few must exploit nature just as it exploits each of us who sell our labour power. We are alienated from nature, and the world is spinning out of our control. It is burning. Some scientists call this stage of history the 'Anthropocene', as if it is the appearance of human beings in the world and their domination of other animals and nature that is the underlying cause of climate change and environmental disaster. It is not.

Human-led destruction is a function of relations of power, of exploitation of nature, of the oppression and alienation that afflicts us all. It has been intensified in the last few hundred years by the capitalist system, so we could really call this period of history the 'Capitalocene'. It is capitalism that is the problem, not human beings. Human beings can work together cooperatively, and will need to do that in order to overthrow capitalism and create better ways to live together.

Domination of nature is at the heart of this, and made central to capitalism as it extracts value from bodies and from the land, extracts it for sale. The drive to dominate nature is sometimes expressed in fear of nature that gets out of control, and sometimes in attempts to 'return' to nature, as if merging with it will solve the problem. That romantic solution, that romanticising of nature will not solve the problem of our alienation from nature. Yes, this is where we should be, with nature, and living alongside other species, and radical psychoanalysis agrees that this is a way forward, while also noticing some of the traps this can lead us into.

Radical psychoanalysis offers a diagnosis of our alienation from nature that is also a diagnosis of the false paths we take when we try to either dominate it or merge with it. We cannot start from scratch, go back to nature, abandon the technical scientific gains we have made. To feed the world and live in these new climate conditions will depend on our rational, collective and democratically-organised abilities. That means confronting our fear of natural forces that are more powerful than us and carefully examining what is possible and what is not. And it means acknowledging that each of us is part of nature, but always transforming it as we make sense of it for ourselves, not being driven by brute animal instincts. We are animal and more than animal, with political responsibility to each other and to the world.

Alienation from creativity

We can change the world we have made: it already has the shape it has. But that is not the whole picture. The world has taken shape guided by the needs of the ruling classes of each epoch, and today by those fuelled by the drive for profit. We do not make the world under conditions of our own choosing. Our creative capacity as human beings, which will enable us to get out of this mess if we act collectively against capitalism, is channelled and distorted by those who buy our labour power and then sell the fruits of our labours.

That is, we are alienated from our creativity. What we creatively produce is stolen from us, and the theft we suffer at the heart of capitalism is even deeper than this. At the very moment that we create something while we work, it is harnessed for sale. What is of value is turned into 'exchange value', into an object that turns our labour into a commodity.

Even our own labour power, even our own bodies, and even elements of nature itself, are turned into commodities by capitalism. Our lives are turned into things for sale – into commodities – and so alienation operates right at the core of what we are as human beings. We are creative beings, living, loving, making sense of this world with others, but that aspect of our human nature is systematically distorted. This systematic distortion, alienation from our creativity, is at the root of much distress, mental distress which is often also expressed through physical distress, real illness.

Psychoanalysis is caught up in this problem, and anyone who has sought help for their distress will know this. When psychoanalysis as a particular kind of treatment of distress is a 'private' treatment, as it so often is, it is also turned into a kind of commodity. The space that someone needs to speak and to be listened to has to be bought, and the professional who offers you that space will be pushed and pulled by market forces. In the public health services, this one-by-one psychoanalytic treatment is expensive, and rationed, and there is a selection of people to be 'patients', usually those who already know how to operate within the rules of the game. Radical psychoanalysis has to be creative, and offer creative solutions, to be up to the task of connecting with change instead of colluding with alienation.

Alienation online

Now, in addition to the other aspects of life that separate us from others and from ourselves, even our forms of communication operate against us. The social media we use to access information about the world is not only unreliable but contradictory, confusing. Interaction online has the effect of drawing us into a gigantic competitive game-like field of communication in which our relationship to reality is systematically undermined. It is as if the real world itself disappears, and in its place are toxic competing messages and images that sometimes bring comfort, a sense of community, but more often bring isolation and anxiety.

One of the claims made by 'humanistic psychotherapists' who mistakenly take our experience at face value is that your feelings are your friends. That was never really true, and 'psychoanalytic psychotherapists' and 'psychoanalysts' argued that we are always separated from our feelings, alienated from them as we try to put them into words. Psychoanalytic 'free association' is a way of noticing that, and noticing how feelings are transformed as we speak about them.

Now, despite the claims of the big media companies who want to sell the latest model of their product to you, your phone is not your friend; it misleads as much as it informs, and it gathers data about you for more marketing, it informs on you. This 'digital alienation' turns your image of yourself online into a commodity to be bought and sold. It is part of a bewitching computerised media universe which gives license to a multitude of conspiracy theories that pretend to give access to a more authentic view of the world while sucking us into an unpleasant destructive meme-world.

Psychoanalysis does not pretend to disclose what the world is really like nor does it disclose what you are really thinking, imagining, fantasising about. Instead, the focus is on the mechanisms by which reality is pushed away, 'repressed'. It is the work of repression that we learn about in psychoanalysis and our relation to our unconscious, not the stuff hidden away in the unconscious or under surface as such.

That is also why radical psychoanalysis is 'ecosocialist' in the sense that it does not return us directly to nature as if that is underneath our human culture, something authentic and deep in which we will feel at home. Rather, radical ecosocialist psychoanalysis helps us together create a world in which we respect other species, respect nature, build a different relationship with it. We live in exile from nature, whereas psychoanalysis helps us live with it.

Separation from life

Radical psychoanalysis provides a critique of alienation that deepens the critical analysis made of capitalism by different political movements. Exploitation of the working class, oppression of women, pathologisation of alternative forms of sexuality – lesbian, gay, bisexual, trans, queer – exclusion of people with disabilities, and the turning of animals into objects only harvested as industrial processed food, all of these aspects of life that produce so much misery are bound together by alienation.

Alienation deepens each aspect of exploitation and oppression under capitalism, and it binds each of us to this society even at the very moments that we want to resist it. We know things are rotten, and we want to speak out, but we often feel afraid, isolated, and helpless. How can we find space to speak, and link that speaking against exploitation and oppression to action? What does psychoanalysis have to say about our creative rebellious energy that would help us give that energy for change a voice, put it to work?

2

What are we?

Separation and conflict are sources of power for those who are already too powerful under capitalism; but they can also be turned into sources of power for ourselves. The system works by 'divide and rule', setting people against each other, inciting them to be good workers who will exclude others, blaming immigrants, women and others. People are made to feel they are missing out, lacking something. They are told they could buy things to make them happy if they could afford to, and that someone or some others are to blame. There are so many traps, traps that lead us to hurt others and hurt ourselves more.

Psychoanalysis provides one way of thinking about what we are, one way of turning separation and conflict into sources of strength. Yes, we need to be able to separate ourselves from our immediate responses to others and ourselves, and we need to be able to do that because those immediate responses are not always the authentic deep feelings that will guide us out of this mess that they pretend to be. This is because 'feelings' under capitalism have also been turned into commodities, objects to be bought and sold, along with every other aspect of life.

Feelings of love, attraction and desire, along with hate, repulsion and resentment, do not flow from our underlying human nature, but are organised by the culture we live in and through which we learn to be human. They are organised under capitalism as part of ideology, ideas that are false, misleading us about how the world works and what our place in it is, telling us that we will always be like this, that things can never change.

Conflict and ambivalence

Political action is one way of separating us from the ruling ideology, the system of ideas that keep the ruling class in place as if their privilege and power was normal and natural. But when we act collectively against capitalism, new ways of living appear as possibilities. Other worlds are possible when we struggle, break from capitalism, and break from the ideology that tells us how we should feel and who we should love and who we should hate, and how we should go about loving and hating.

It is not possible to have political action without conflict, conflict between classes, conflict between ideas about how the world could and should be organised, and here psychoanalysis emphasises a key element of change. For psychoanalysis, conflict is always present in every social relationship, whether at the level of society or at the level of organisations or groups, including inside every family, whatever form that family takes. And, crucially, conflict is always present inside each individual.

We are taught to be 'individuals' under capitalism, and this means two things; that we are separate from others, 'individuated' from them instead of working with them collectively; and that we are 'undivided', operating as if we are complete self-contained units. But neither of these things is true: we are always linked to others and we are always divided beings.

We are all riddled with conflict. We are divided from ourselves, wanting and not wanting the same thing at the same time, and wanting different things that pull us in different directions. We sometimes hate those we love, we feel torn about what we are told we need and what we think we need. In psychoanalytic terms we are *ambivalent*, always ambivalent, contradictory beings.

That contradictoriness, that ambivalence, fires change, it opens the way to noticing what can be different, leads us to act so that we make a difference in the world. When it finds expression in the political realm, when it becomes anti-capitalist, that ambivalence and the creative engagement in conflict that goes with it enables us to see that every radical political movement is also divided, and that its internal division need not be a source of weakness but can be a source of strength.

That is why times of revolution, when social

conflicts come out into the open and there is a possibility of changing the world, perhaps of overthrowing capitalism, are so energising. Times of revolution make visible different kinds of conflict, not only around class relations but also around questions of gender, sexuality and what minority groups are able to say and do.

Repression and freedom

Repressive regimes hate psychoanalysis as well as radical politics. This was the case for the fascist regimes in Europe, and that is why psychoanalysts had to flee for their lives from the Nazis, and it was also the case for the Stalinist regimes in the Soviet bloc. Those regimes were threatened by class conflict, and by the struggles of women and minority communities, and they were threatened by psychoanalysis as an approach to our internal lives that emphasises the role of conflict.

Russia under Stalin and the other regimes modelled on the Soviet Union forbade psychoanalysis, and there is a political question for us here about what form radical politics must take. It must always be committed to democratic rights. The fundamental method of psychoanalysis as a treatment of distress is 'free association', to speak as freely as possible about ideas that come to mind, ideas that are associated with our distress. It is through that free association that it is possible to get a sense of how we have been formed as individuals, each one of us thinking about some particular things that bewitch or bother us and refusing to think about other things.

Free association is a method that enables us to notice the form alienation takes for each person. Of course, free association inside psychoanalysis requires freedom of speech in society. Just as free association inside psychoanalysis brings to light repressed ideas about sexuality and the choices we make about how to love, so free association in the political realm is the necessary space for the creative flowering of ideas about new forms of identity, including sexual identity, lesbian, gay, bisexual, trans, queer and so on.

New forms of identity open up new ways of connecting with oppressed groups, new more open relations between different cultural communities.

So, a society that has forbidden freedom of speech will be suspicious of what might be spoken about inside psychoanalysis in case it spills out into the open.

Fascism

Fascism is a particularly dangerous case in point, and particularly dangerous now when there are new fascist movements. Fascism grows when there is conflict that gets out of control, out of control of the ruling class and the capitalist state that is dedicated to protecting large-scale private property, private corporations, and the power of the ruling class. Fascism takes power when the working class and other movements of the oppressed have failed, when they are beaten, when they are weak. Then the role of fascism is to restore order, to ensure there is no internal conflict, and to enable profits to rise.

Before it takes power, fascism is a deadly enemy of free association and an enemy of any genuinely liberating political movements that open up conflict. The way fascism deals with conflict is quite specific, and dangerous. It replaces internal conflict with conflict directed at others, at those who are different.

Fascism combines two forms of repression: direct repression by the capitalist state through assassination, abduction, arrest and imprisonment; and ideological repression through an ideological assault on the very idea of free association. It is that ideological repression working its way into the mind of each individual that has been the main concern of psychoanalysis. It is radical psychoanalysis that speaks explicitly of these things.

Fascism mobilises and intensifies the fear each of us have about our alienated lives and what might happen if we start to think about the possibility that things could be different. The fear is harnessed into what psychoanalysis calls 'defences'. We can think here of the way the capitalist state defends itself by setting fascism loose at times of threat, and of internal defences as how that process replicates itself inside the individual so they stop themselves thinking, and then hate what they perceive to be different.

This is how conflict inside society which might

lead to revolutionary transformation, to the end of capitalism and to the flowering of different ways of being human, is replaced by fascism, with the kind of controlled conflict which gathers together a people as if they are all the same and pits them against those who are different. The mass murder of people diagnosed as having 'mental illness', of disabled people, of homosexuals, and of Jews and Roma and other minorities under the Nazis was a gigantic horrific cleansing of society of real conflict. There was an ideological assault on those who were marked as different and an ideological fantasy that by wiping out conflict the society could function as some kind of healthy natural organism.

There is so much psychoanalytic writing on fascism precisely because it is a telling example of how the simple enforcement of 'health' can be so sick, so destructive. Radical psychoanalysis values difference and speaking about it, and living it, and psychoanalysis was a target of fascism for that very reason.

History and fantasy

Fascism and other reactionary political forces – those designed to block anti-capitalist and liberation movements – are driven by a fantasy about what is normal and natural in society. This means they are also driven by a fantasy that wipes away history. Fantasy is a kind of organised illusion that feels comforting but can sometimes be disturbing and dangerous, be delusory. This fantasy can be understood as being a necessary part of the ruling ideology of capitalist societies; it takes different forms in different capitalist societies but boils down to the same claim, that this social order is how we always were and must always be.

Psychoanalysis looks at how ideological fantasy operates at a deeper level, inside each individual, who uses those attempts to wipe away history to shore up their own sense of self, their own fragile ego. The thought that we were not always like this and that things may change is unbearable to those whose lives and societies are ruled by fantasy, those who rely on many different kinds of 'defence' to forbid other possibilities being thought or talked about.

The fact is that capitalism has only been the dominant system of political-economic rule on this planet for quite a short time, a few hundred years, and in some countries it is even less than that. The development of capitalism in Europe required the 'under-development' of other parts of the world, with natural resources plundered and peoples enslaved. Colonialism meant racist regimes of white people who treated those they ruled as lesser beings, to be repressed and prevented from speaking and acting for themselves.

This was a feature of capitalism from the beginning. Each capitalist culture has its own peculiar way of 'inventing tradition', that is, making it seem as if quite recent ways of living were always there, as if they had existed back into the mists of time.

It simply is not true that national cultures always existed as they do now. National cultures invent their history to operate in the present and hold things in place. One of the insights of psychoanalysis is that the stories each of us tell ourselves about who we are operate in the same kind of way. We are told and told again who we are and what our family and cultural allegiances should be as if they are normal and natural.

Stories we tell ourselves about who and how we should love, how our sexual enjoyment is organised, are of a piece with that. Not only are they fictions, as fictional as the supposedly conflict-free nationalist and fascist stories about the past, but these fantasies wipe away the real history of how we have come to be who we are.

Psychoanalysis warns us that we cannot ever travel back in time to be sure of the real story, what really happened, but we can question the stories that have been handed down to us and that rule our lives. New stories can be invented, but they need new conditions of life for that to happen. Conflict, and the tension between different stories, opens up the possibility that we might remake ourselves, and radical psychoanalysis helps us think about how we might remake ourselves at a personal level while remaking ourselves together with others at a collective level.

3

Where is psychoanalysis now?

Psychoanalysis also has a history. Some psychoanalysts think that it was 'discovered' by Sigmund Freud at the end of the nineteenth century, so they are caught up in their own quite un-psychoanalytic way of wishing away the history of the world before Freud. To insist that it was 'discovered' is to make it seem that it was always there, and it was the lucky break of this guy in Vienna to hit upon it, dig it up.

The problem is that to assume psychoanalysis was always there leads to a-historical stories of the past, and to attempts to apply psychoanalytic ideas to pre-capitalist times where it makes no sense. It also leads to the idea that we will never be free of psychoanalysis, and to a colonialist assumption that every other culture can be psychoanalysed. Radical psychoanalysts are more careful and say instead that psychoanalysis was 'invented' by Freud and his followers.

Psychoanalysis was invented at a time when it made perfect sense. Freud himself often liked to claim that psychoanalysis was scientific, and tried to apply it to historical figures as if it would work as an explanatory framework for the past as well as for the present under capitalism. But actually, like Marxism, which is specifically designed to understand and challenge capitalist society, psychoanalysis is specifically geared to understand the society it was invented in. This was a developing capitalist society in which there was increasing alienation, and so the increasing separation of individuals from each other. Then it made sense that distress that is experienced at an individual level should be treated at an individual level. The distress and the treatment are thus 'privatised'. Psychoanalysis speaks of life in and against capitalist society.

The alienation of people from their own bodies was the context for the weird 'hysterical' symptoms that patients came to Freud with; bits of their bodies were operating separately from their owners, shouting, twitching, convulsing, or paralysed. These patients' own nature was a threat to them, and their own creative capacities were systematically distorted. Collective activity was also seen as a threat, as a kind of pathology, and that was an idea about groups and crowds that Freud himself, who was a political liberal who worried about radical and rapid social change, actively supported.

This is not at all to say that capitalism alone was the only cause or context for the development of psychoanalysis. The treatment of women as emotional non-rational beings also meant that the kind of psychoanalysis that wanted to be a 'science' then sided with stereotypically dominant masculinity, sided with men at the head of the patriarchal family. Patriarchy is the organised power of men over women, with the family as a crucial relay point for that power. The development of capitalism in Europe, which was intimately linked with the exploitation of the rest of the world, meant that images of 'civilisation' and of 'savages' who were seen as a threat played a key role in Freud's own ideas about child 'development'.

Freud, as a Jew, and therefore marginal to mainstream capitalist society because of antisemitism, was certainly critical of society, but he was also trained as a psychiatrist, a medical professional anxious about his own status. So, when it came down to it, he sided with this society against those who argued for a different way of being that would really have enabled people to live their own lives, perhaps a little more free of repression.

Now, as a consequence of this history, we have a problem. The problem is that psychoanalysis is a key to unlock some aspects of capitalist society, but it is also the lock, part of the very society it gives critical insight into. This is where things get complicated, where we really need a political understanding of psychoanalysis too.

Academic psychoanalysis

One problem of psychoanalysis is that there is so much of it in the academic world. One of the consequences of the destruction of psychoanalysis by the Nazis in Germany was that when psychoanalysts fled and found new homes in other countries, they were understandably anxious about their immigrant status and concerned about 'adapting themselves' to their new homes. In the process many of them turned psychoanalysis from being a tool of critique and rebellion into a tool of adaptation, focused on fitting people in and enabling them to behave as good, well-behaved citizens in a capitalist culture.

Some psychoanalysts stayed critical, and new waves of psychoanalysis, particularly in the English-speaking world, have taken root in university departments. However, 'critical' academic work is often very different from real political critique linked to action. To really critically analyse capitalism, or racism or sexism, should be to provide a radical interpretation that empowers people to change things. More than that, the very act of reading and taking seriously a critical analysis of society should involve the reader in a process of political change, and the test of the analysis will be the process of collective change they engage in, through strikes, occupations, and constructions of new forms of life that challenge the capitalist state.

Academics are trained to read and write, and to publish in journals that are read by other academics, and 'popular' books about their research are often frowned on in their own departments. Research projects are usually funded by organisations that want to limit the 'impact' of the research to future 'social policy'. This means that the kind of psychoanalysis that has become popular in departments of literature or philosophy or psychology and even in 'social theory' or politics has adapted itself to those niches. It then becomes rather abstract, even elitist, and is often incomprehensible to people who live and work and want to change the real world.

There have been some interesting critical psychoanalytic analyses of fascism, however, and some of the émigrés from continental Europe who found homes elsewhere in university departments provide some insights into the nature of fascism. More recently, some of the new developments in theories of sexuality, most notably queer theory, have happened in these departments. It is to the credit of the academics who have reached out and tried to connect those theories with changes in the real world that they have broken with traditional academic practice, broken through traditional academic boundaries.

Clinical psychoanalysis

In this process, and again this is particularly the case in the English-speaking world, the radical psychoanalysis that has developed in academic departments has often been disconnected from psychoanalysis in the clinic.

In the clinical realm – where psychoanalysis is used as a treatment of distress – psychoanalysis is sometimes confused with psychiatry. Psychiatry is a medical profession, and even when psychiatrists turn their hand to talking about problems with their patients, there is still, at the back of their minds, a medical understanding of the symptom as the expression of some kind of disorder, as an illness. Freud was trained as a psychiatrist and had to break from it in order to develop psychoanalysis. Psychoanalysis is not a medical treatment: it is a talking cure.

If you put things into words, that does not guarantee that you will be listened to without being judged; but that is what a psychoanalyst should do. A psychoanalyst listens, draws attention to contradictions, repetitions, opens up conflict in order to work with it and understand what is going on, and, most importantly, makes space for their patient to understand for themselves what is going on. The talking is to another, and the other person, the psychoanalyst, does challenge, does draw attention to the repetitions, does not let the person who speaks to them off the hook so they can pretend that things are just running as normal, as if there is no contradiction, as if there is no conflict.

The kind of professional who does judge and lead the patient along a certain path is usually someone schooled in psychology. Psychology is devoted to noticing problematic thoughts and putting them right, so there are often underlying assumptions about what is normal and what is abnormal.

Here we are back to the problem of judging and setting out how people should be happy, how they should function in society. Radical psychoanalysis is effectively a form of 'anti-psychology'.

Often psychoanalysis provides insight in the clinic that is therapeutic, but psychoanalysts are very careful not to rush too fast, to simply make the therapy the be-all and end-all of the treatment. Understanding, which is a priority for psychotherapists who want to make you feel you have been understood, has a role, but so does misunderstanding, which is much more important for radical psychoanalysis. Understanding too-often functions to draw people into the same frame as the psychotherapist. Parents like to say to their children that they 'understand' them, but it is better when they can tolerate misunderstanding.

Psychoanalysts tolerate and work with misunderstanding, their own and that of the analysand, who encounters their own unconscious as they speak. A psychoanalyst should know that every individual has their own singular way of dealing with alienation, with making their symptoms work for them, and that giving them a space to speak is not the same as pretending to 'understand' the inner life of another human being.

Freud is sometimes quoted as saying that the function of psychoanalysis is to transform hysterical misery into ordinary unhappiness. How could psychoanalysis pretend to do more than that in a society that is systematically organised around exploitation and oppression? Unhappiness and the selling of commodities that pretend to make people 'happy' is the name of the game under capitalism. We can only claim more than Freud did for psychoanalysis by linking psychoanalysis with social change, with ending this wretched political-economic system once and for all.

Psychoanalysis is all around us

We are all familiar with images of psychoanalysts sitting behind a couch and of patients babbling on about their childhoods to no good effect, except that they end up blaming their parents for their problems and then idealise psychoanalysis, maybe training to be an analyst or giving amateur interpretations to their friends and comrades about the 'Oedipus complex' or some other idea they have picked up. We might have heard about the Oedipus complex as a description of rivalry with dad and desire to marry mum, and the pity of it is that some enthusiasts for psychoanalysis use this to interpret whole societies. At least in the clinic we know that the aim is not to make people fit into the so-called Oedipus complex but to free them from it.

What we face here is the popular cultural uptake of psychoanalytic ideas. That makes the task of explaining how psychoanalysis can be 'radical' a very difficult one. On the one hand, if we make things too simple, then we just play along with everyday commonsense about our unconscious lives or the role of fantasy, and then we have explained nothing. Things stay in place, nothing changes. On the other hand, if we make things too complicated, we come across as some kind of crank, or as a 'psy' professional peddling their interpretations, or as an academic turning politics into some kind of weird thesis.

There is a risk here also in using psychoanalytic

ideas in the anti-capitalist movement. There has long been a close link between psychoanalysis and the left. Some of the most radical figures on the revolutionary left have been attracted to psychoanalysis; it kind of plugs in a gap in political analysis about the role of the individual in history, and it does help explain why people remain so attached to irrational ideas that are actually so obviously reactionary and self-sabotaging.

There has also been an uptake of psychoanalytic ideas among feminists who can use it to unravel the claims of patriarchy to show us what is 'normal' and 'natural' about sexuality, and this does take us in the direction of radical psychoanalysis. Psychoanalysis in the hands of feminists opens the way to a really queer sexuality that is revolutionary, against what is assumed to be 'normal'. No one is 'normal'.

In anti-colonial and anti-racist theory, there has also been use of psychoanalysis to understand racism, not only racism of the oppressors, how they defend themselves against people who are different, but also internalised racism among the oppressed. Psychoanalysis is very good at showing how all of us buy into our oppression.

We sometimes find pop psychoanalytic ideas appear in the left and feminist and anti-colonial movements, in the notion that unconscious urges that have been 'repressed' and so should be released, for example, or that there are really healthy kinds of sexuality that need to be expressed as part of the revolution.

We do not 'release' or 'express' stuff in a revolution: we *create* it. Our task is to build a revolutionary movement and lay the basis for the creating a better world beyond capitalism. We need to beware of the way that psychoanalysis is tamed, and turned into part of the ideological apparatus of capitalism. Sometimes the distortions of psychoanalysis are relatively innocent, but we need to tread with care, and not listen to one individual guru or another telling us what is what.

Psychoanalysis teaches us to be sceptical about masters or claims to mastery or master-frameworks that pretend to explain anything and everything. We should already have learned the dangers of that from the degeneration of Marxism into something akin to a religious faith under Stalin and in the apparently 'post-capitalist' workers' states. The development of radical psychoanalysis will change from context to context, and must be a collective process.

4

What use is it?

This is the crunch point. What use can be made of psychoanalysis in practice in a way that works with revolutionary movements instead of against them? For all the progressive ideas and practical possibilities that Freud and his followers opened up, there are lots of traps. Like many other radical ideas, psychoanalysis has been absorbed and neutralised, turned against us even while it points towards liberation. So here we will look at psychoanalytic ideas in practice in three domains, that of the individual, the group, and society as a whole, and point to what these ideas offer and some of the dangers we need to beware of.

IAN PARKER

Science of struggle and transformation

Psychoanalysis is 'scientific' in a special way that is connected with its practice. It is not a 'natural science' like chemistry or physics, but a human science; that is, it provides an explanatory framework for understanding the social world. When it pretends to be neutral and 'objective' like a natural science and simply circulates as a set of ideas that are disconnected from practice, there is a real risk that it turns into ideology, into false ideas that present the world as unchangeable, that present the domination and power we suffer as natural and unchangeable.

Then the danger is that psychoanalysis turns into some kind of weird worldview that pretends to explain everything; then it makes a bid to be a kind of 'master code' that will unlock all the puzzles of the social and natural world. Some psychoanalysts are drawn into that way of thinking, and they are then resistant to, even hostile towards, other forms of knowledge. They may lecture feminists and Marxists about what they have got wrong and busy themselves putting psychoanalytic ideas in place of liberating ones.

But the best of radical psychoanalysis is actually closer to Marxism and feminism. Marxism is not just a theory to describe the world, still less to guide 'policy-makers' to help capitalism run more smoothly, or to prop up a regime that uses Marxism as some sort of religious faith. That was how it came to function in Russia, and does still now in China, both capitalist countries.

Marxism is geared to transform the world at the very same moment that it explains what exploitation and oppression is. Marxism makes sense from the standpoint of the exploited, not from the standpoint of those with power, whether those are businesspersons or politicians. It makes sense because it transforms our understanding and impels us into action to change the world. Then, in the process of changing social conditions, we can test out best which aspects work for us. Feminism and the most radical forms of sexual politics, and antiracist struggle too, similarly work as a process of change. The process of change uncovers what has been holding us back. They are sciences of struggle, of transformation.

This is why radical psychoanalysis is a science of struggle and transformation; it is part of a struggle to understand how we have come to be who we are at a personal level and it aids transformation of ourselves as we engage in that process of understanding. This means that the theory does not work when it is simply handed down to people, when they are told what they must think, but only when they think and act for themselves. Just as Marxist and feminist and anti-racist ideas must be put into practice by the exploited and oppressed, by themselves and for themselves as they become conscious of what this world is doing to them, so psychoanalysis is a means for someone to think and act for themselves.

Sometimes this person who makes use of psychoanalysis is called a 'patient', as if psychoanalysis is a medical profession, or a 'client', as if they are buying a service. In psychoanalytic jargon this person is termed 'analysand'; an 'analysand' is the one who analyses. It is not the only path, the only approach, but it is a useful one. How might it work?

Personal as political

We experience ourselves as separate beings in capitalist society because we have been brought up to compete with others, and that also means that we experience our distress at an individual level. Political activists are faced with distress about the horrible things that are done to them at an individual level, and this distress is compounded by their awareness of exploitation and oppression. This has always been the case, and activists have had to care for themselves, seek out support, while carrying on struggling alongside others in social movements and radical groups. They know that collective work is the only thing that will make a difference, but this is not easy, sometimes painful, sometimes too much to bear.

We see this today among our comrades and people new to political struggle who are shocked, horrified, overwhelmed by the scale of abuse and violence in the world. Many people who are finding out about the climate catastrophe, the destruction of the world as a result of the drive for profit, violence against women and endemic racism can feel that it is easier to imagine the end of the world than the end of capitalism. We see this among our sisters and brothers who are attempting to make sense of the way their bodies are impacted by sexism, and when they explore what it means to be male or female, queer or trans, they are subject to abuse by family and friends and even by some on the left, by those who should know better.

Not only have we hard lessons to learn about the depth of hurt caused by racism and the treatment of people who are disabled – disabled because their bodies are not seen as fit to make them productive workers – but we have lessons to learn about how to respond to distress.

Distress, like much else in this world, is 'privatised', locked inside us. That means that it makes perfect sense for us to try and buy a service that will help us feel better, to ask for help as a 'client' or a consumer. And it sometimes makes sense for us to believe that our distress is because of some medical problem – so we seek out a mind doctor and turn ourselves into 'patients'.

There are many responses we need to learn from, many of which are not psychoanalytic at all. These include those who can see that 'mental distress' is privatised and look to collective solutions through refusing medical diagnoses or treatments that aim to make them think differently and adapt them to a sick world. There are movements for 'mad pride' that do this, and movements that give space for people to talk about the way they harm themselves, or their experience of hearing voices, or their paranoia, or their need to rebel.

Psychiatric labels sometimes give people comfort and access to support, but these labels need to be redefined and used by people themselves if they must be used at all, not handed down as a kind of medical life-sentence by a doctor or by a family that has bought into a medical explanation as a quick fix. Some 'anti-psychiatry' movements argue that when we are labelled as 'ill' we need to respond by turning around that label and treat illness as a weapon, to channel our rage in collective struggle.

Psychoanalysis also needs to learn from these approaches and needs to ally with them. But what does psychoanalysis do that is different in what psychoanalysts still like to call the 'clinic'? This psychoanalytic 'clinic' is not run by men in white coats, but is simply a confidential space in which we speak to another person – speak to the psychoanalyst or psychoanalytic therapist or psychodynamic counsellor, or in a 'group analytic' meeting – and encounter something of ourselves that we usually push away, make 'unconscious'. Psychoanalysis is a 'talking cure'. That description was used by one of the first analysands.

Does the analysand lie on a couch? Maybe. What is important is that they are given confidential safe space to speak without being judged. Psychoanalysts should not push interpretations, but give space for the analysand to analyse. Yes, the psychoanalyst notices repetition of key words or phrases, and notices how significant relationships with other key figures are repeated, including in relation to them as analyst.

They are repeated, noticed, and the analysand can then decide to move on. This decision is difficult. The joke goes that it only takes one psychotherapist to change a light-bulb but the light-bulb must really want to change.

This joke does not work if you take psychoanalysis seriously because we are so locked into who we have been told we are that we put a lot of effort into preventing change. The light-bulb analysand does not want to change, they want things to stay the same. It is easier to stay stuck and just repeat what you have always said and done, so this analysis that happens in the presence of a psychoanalyst who incites change, and enables change, is difficult, sometimes annoying, upsetting.

Now we have another warning, which is that some psychoanalysts are medically trained, so they cannot help themselves diagnosing and then giving interpretations, as if interpreting was a kind of medicine. This is the way of some psychoanalysts who 'treat' trans as if it was all a matter of what medically-trained professionals call 'dysphoria'. Sometimes it is worse, and the psychoanalyst carries into their clinic reactionary ideas about supposedly natural biological differences between men and women. Sometimes they bring in well-meaning ideas they have learnt about different cultures, so they end up making assumptions that are racist. Sometimes they are just downright conservative, and then they have bought into the idea that people must change instead of changing the world.

These problems are made worse by the way that much psychoanalysis takes place as private practice outside the NHS, so analysands have to pay, and the psychoanalyst comes to believe that it is important that they pay in order to make the cure take place. And, inside the NHS, the psychoanalysts often work in a medical institution, with 'assessment' and 'diagnosis' and 'treatment' turning the talking cure into a trap rather than a way out of our misery.

We must take seriously the feminist slogan that the 'personal is political' by working with 'personal' and privatised distress as something political. Radical psychoanalysis does not reduce politics to the personal level, but embeds what psychoanalysts do in a political understanding of individual distress, of why it takes shape as something individual. Radical psychoanalysts work in alliance with other movements tackling the reality of distress, and they have a political understanding of the contexts and institutions in which the talking cure can be helpful.

Groups and organisations

We must organise collectively, join political groups, and work together if we are to change the world. Individual-enclosed 'change' is not enough, and is actually quite impossible in a world that is structured to reward competition and pathologise those who are different, those who cannot or will not fit in.

But groups and organisations and political parties are also, of course, riddled with problems. It could not be otherwise. They cannot avoid carrying in aspects of racism and sexism and unthinking reactionary ideas from the outside world. They struggle against the world as it is but they also replicate it. Sometimes that is because of the personal problems that individuals bring into the group and play out there, and sometimes it is because of the peculiar way that groups work.

We are sometimes faced with places that should be liberating but actually feel suffocating. The groups sometimes operate as exhausting institutions that drain our energy instead of inspiring us. Meetings become taken up with deadly boring procedures in which the same things seem to be repeated without anything changing, with the same people dominating the discussion. Then there is a sense of futility, hopelessness. Even, in some cases, the group has a power structure than enables men to take advantage and harass or abuse women. This has happened in some left parties. Then there is understandable hostility to the idea of joining a political party at all. People burnt by the group turn in on themselves; they retreat, leave, and nothing has been learned.

The most radical psychoanalysis sometimes takes the form of 'group analysis' or the application of group psychotherapeutic ideas to understand better how these organisations do this to us, how they get away with it. The task, as with individual psychoanalysis, is not to make people adapt or to simply make the organisation function more 'efficiently', but to notice what it is doing to people and how they might work better – better according to their own collectively-decided criteria instead of according to the expert imposing their own ideas.

The psychoanalyst might help us notice how

'defences' are operating in a group so that certain ideas are avoided, repeatedly pushed away. To talk about racism in an organisation, for example, makes people feel uncomfortable, so one way the members 'defend' themselves is to avoid talking about it, or even worse, to label those who do want to talk about it as obsessed or as trouble-makers.

Sex and sexuality in organisations are often flashpoints because sex and sexuality feel so intimate, a private space, and we energetically protect it, and feel all the more violated when those with power abuse us. Psychoanalysts notice how 'splitting' works to divide the good people we are willing to listen to from the bad people we want to avoid. We notice how people seem driven to 'split', unable to weigh up ideas rationally, but tending to strike out. Sometimes there are fantasy forms of defence, in which the organisation develops a sense of itself as some kind of invulnerable or super-important thing, and then splitting is all the more dangerous, because those who are marginalised are accused of sabotaging what has been built. Never underestimate the power of the unconscious in an organisation, but also, at the same time, give space to take seriously what the real obstacles to changing things are.

Here again there is a problem and a warning about the use of psychoanalytic ideas. This is to do with the kind of knowledge that psychoanalysts develop to protect themselves. They are very skilled at turning everything into their own kind of knowledge. This means that when we listen to them we need to be able to embed what they are saying about unconscious processes and unthinking repetition and so on in a political context. We can make use of psychoanalysis, but it is politics that must be the priority in order to bring about social change.

There is time for reflection on what is happening in an organisation – and we need that time – and there is time for action, when we put ideas into practice. A group can take seriously psychoanalytic insights without wallowing in continual talk about how 'hurt' it feels or reducing things to the personal pathologies of its members. Whatever, the group must think about what it is doing, and psychoanalysis can be of assistance.

Society, culture, ideology

We are trying to change the world, and we know that only by working as internationalists can we make a difference. We have learned from bitter experience that there can be no 'socialism in one country', but our fate in the world is tied to the fate of other people divided into different 'nations' and so-called 'races'. Even less can we build socialism inside one individual, which is the kind of illusion of personal responsibility that some non-psychoanalytic psychotherapists fuel. Solidarity in struggle is what embeds what we do at a local level at every point in what is happening at a global level. That struggle is material and it is ideological, so we need to understand something about culture, local and global, and intervene in that. Psychoanalysis is one way of understanding and intervening.

Fascism and creeping fascism is one pressing example of a political process that psychoanalysis helps us to understand. We need a political analysis of the way that fascism appears at times of defeat and demoralisation of the working class, how fascism takes root in the middle class trapped between the power of the big capitalists and the working-class organisations. But the poisonous resentment of fascism, directed at those perceived to be 'different', has a dimension of irrationality that we need to grasp. Sexual freedom and the self-assertion of cultural minorities enrage the fascists, and fascism as a brutal social phenomenon entails a violent 'repression' that operates at an emotional level as well as at a directly political-state level.

For fascism, liberation of the variety of ways of being human in this world is a threat, and fascist anger then hooks into and feeds dangerous paranoiac fantasies about conspiracies and hidden puppet-masters pulling the strings behind the scenes. As well as 'projecting' their anger and resentment onto others – and that is so they then experience that anger and resentment as coming from others instead of from themselves – fascists split the world into good and bad. The crazy QAnon theory is a good example. It feeds into contemporary fascism and images of George Soros as one of the Jewish puppet-masters.

Those viewed as the bad are then turned into scapegoats; with antisemitic anger and then fear following projection often focused on Jews, harnessing long-standing conspiracy theories peddled by the right, also against Muslims in the Islamophobic fantasy of 'race-mixing'. Fascists like things to be pure, wholesome, ordered, and their fantasy of 'race-mixing' taps into their deepest irrational fears. Fascism is not the kind of problem that can be understood by psychologists or a 'mental illness' cured by psychiatrists, and although psychoanalysis does show us how some bizarre pathological self-destructive things go on for people drawn to fascism, it does not reduce fascism as a political problem to personal pathology.

So here we need to take care, and here is another warning. Psychoanalysis discloses something of what is happening in right-wing ideology, but that right-wing ideology also operates on its own, independently of the 'unconscious' mental processes that psychoanalysis focuses on. So, again, we have to remember not to let psychoanalysis reduce everything to its own domain of expertise, to what it describes of the internal world. There was antisemitism before psychoanalysis, and that toxic ideological phenomenon shadowed the profession, labelling it, under the Nazis, a 'Jewish science'.

There is another problem which is that psychoanalysis often pretends to be neutral, objective, pretends to be the kind of science that simply describes the world instead of changing it. Those psychoanalysts who offer themselves as interpreters of culture then forget a key point from psychoanalytic practice, which is that it is the analysand who analyses, not the psychoanalyst. Many different things are happening for different individuals and groups in society that cannot be 'interpreted' psychoanalytically so easily, and we need to engage in reflection on what is driving us for ourselves. Psychoanalysts often forget this in their enthusiasm to explain what is happening in their own terms, and then conservative psychoanalysts try to 'balance' their analysis of cultural phenomena and end up advocating 'balance' as the most sensible response to what they view as irrational and 'extremist' responses to the world.

'Extremism' is not the problem. We do need to take extreme steps to get out us of this awful world. We revolutionaries are extremists; we hate what capitalism has done to us and our planet, and we are committed to mobilising people collectively to change the world. Another world is possible, and we will need to act to bring that about, peacefully if we may, but defending ourselves physically if we must, as exploited and oppressed people have done throughout history. We do not 'balance' right-wing and left-wing ideas as if we are the BBC, for we are committed to anti-capitalist struggle in alliance with anti-racists, feminists, and disability-rights activists. We take our stand always against the oppressor and with the oppressed.

Sometimes that means we take sides against psychoanalysis that merely offers 'explanations' and then operates as a form of ideology. Psychoanalysis has been marginal, even repressed in different parts of the world during the century since Freud invented it, but we face a more complicated situation now. Psychoanalysis is also part of popular culture. For some people it is part of their commonsense; they talk about the 'unconscious' and 'fantasy' and 'splitting' and 'projection'. We see images around us in film and television of analysands lying on couches or psychoanalysts giving interpretations, and Freudian ideas have become part of middle-class chatter. This can have the effect of dissolving politics into psychoanalysis, reducing social conflicts into individual conflicts.

5

What can we make of it?

Psychoanalysis is not the only radical approach to our distress under capitalism. We need to take it seriously, but to be as 'intersectional' in our use of it as we are in our linking together of different kinds of revolutionary politics. Intersectionality is an approach to revolutionary politics that links together different standpoints from within the field of the exploited and oppressed, valuing each standpoint or claim to identity in order to throw light on what is missing in the others.

We draw attention to each dimension of oppression not in order to prioritise any particular identity, a sense of who we are, but to show how we construct new identities in alliance, in political action. Traditional anti-capitalist class politics often carries with it racism and sexism, for instance, but anti-racist and feminist struggle enrich that politics. It is self-critical, energising. Identities are important here, but so are the connections, the links, the spaces between any one particular identity, whether as woman or man, or black or white, or working class or 'middle class'.

Psychoanalysis gives an account of the development of personal identity that is already, in some senses, 'intersectional'. We think we are this or that, when we are in fact patched together from different relationships we have forged with significant others in the course of our lives; our individual 'ego' is the product of many competing 'identifications', emotionally-charged connections with and images of others important to us. The competing attachments we have remain with us at an unconscious level, and there are conflicts between them. The conflicts and contradictions give us space for movement. They are the stuff of change, necessary to it. This is the 'ambivalence' that we described earlier as fuelling possibilities of change.

Local and global

Psychoanalysis works at the contradictory connection between the 'personal' and the 'political'. By 'political' we mean the realm of collective struggle that we learn from as we attempt to change things – something very different from the bureaucratic, alienating world of professional politics. And by 'personal' we mean the emotional, experiential engagement we have with change and with our comrades as we struggle – something very different from burrowing away into therapy and trying to change ourselves instead of changing the world.

That means that we work at a local level, very local, even down into the individual when necessary, giving space for things to be worked through. That space may take the form of what we think of as the 'clinic', but this clinic can be a safe, confidential, secure space, while also being a space that is clearly and explicitly connected with the broader process of political change.

And it means that we work at the wider social level, and here it is important that those working with psychoanalysis learn from the social movements they are part of, learn about the limitations of psychoanalysis. At the broadest level, it means that this radical psychoanalysis must be internationalist, learning from the work of other radical movements that have encountered psychoanalysis, learning what they have made of it.

The argument we are making here about the possible progressive role of psychoanalysis has been made many times before in different ways. There were Marxists among the psychoanalysts in central Europe in the 1920s who focused on the link between political repression, repression in the nuclear family and sexual repression, and who tried to harness energies for change. Revolutionaries were attracted to psychoanalysis in the 1930s, when fascism was growing; they found in it a way to explain the power of fantasy in distorting people's desire for change and making them hate difference instead of embracing it.

Émigré psychoanalysts tried to keep radical ideas in psychoanalysis alive in the 1940s and 1950s in the different contexts they worked in around the world. In the 1950s and 1960s anti-colonial psychoanalysts were part of national liberation movements that worked with and challenged the depth and hold of racism. Feminists looked to psychoanalysis in the 1960s and 1970s to understand how patriarchy – the power of men over women – was operating at the level of fantasy as part of capitalism. We have seen fresh waves of LGBTQI+ interest in psychoanalysis because it offers a new way to understand 'identity' and 'identity politics' and to find a way through that to collective struggle.

There are surprising examples from around the world already, ranging from the emergence of 'free clinics' in the favelas of Brazil, where radical psychoanalysts listen and support people in communities without imposing their theory as a model of the world, to the psychoanalytic work in Palestine, where practitioners build the self-confidence of a people speaking and acting against occupation.

In Brazil there are psychoanalysts who have been publicly active in the struggle against the creeping fascism of Jair Bolsonaro, who not only burns the rainforests and denies the existence of coronavirus, which is affecting the poorest people most, and, not surprisingly, is hostile to anything about sexuality that breaks from the standard 'normal' nuclear family. Psychoanalysts stand in elections with the radical left parties, and psychoanalysts are part of the lesbian, gay, bisexual, trans, and queer movements.

In Palestine there are psychoanalysts who are building resistance to the occupation of land and minds by the Israeli state. This means strengthening bonds of solidarity and a collective sense of the power of the Palestinian people, while also resisting the reactionary use of psychoanalytic ideas that pathologise the Palestinians for daring to resist. These radical psychoanalysts offer a powerful critique of the idea of 'balance' and the attempt to dissolve political struggle into 'dialogue' that would label those who resist as being dangerous, fanatical 'extremists'.

The development of radical psychoanalysis will be in conditions of dialogue and joint action with these and many other initiatives, and we will be searching for ways to speak and act against alienation and exploitation and oppression, searching for other worlds within and for another world that we build together in the future.

FURTHER READING

For a deeper dive into some of the ideas that went into this pamphlet, here are five great books:

Arruzza, C. (2013) *Dangerous Liaisons: The Marriages and Divorces of Marxism and Feminism*. London: Resistance Books. [Cinzia Arruzza, an Italian feminist and revolutionary, gives a clear account of the many different ways that feminists and Marxists link together in theory and practice, including 'queer' and psychoanalytic perspectives]

Fanon, F. (2017) *Black Skin, White Masks*. London: Pluto. [Frantz Fanon, an Algerian anti-colonial revolutionary and radical psychiatrist originally from Martinique, drew on psychoanalytic ideas to discuss racism in this classic book, and the way that oppression works its way into the lives of the oppressed]

Gherovici, P. (2017) *Transgender Psychoanalysis: A Lacanian Perspective on Sexual Difference*. London and New York: Routledge. [Patricia Gherovici, a practising psychoanalyst from Argentina, shows how psychoanalysis can learn from the experience of trans in order to make clinical work welcoming and transformative]

Pavón Cuéllar, D. (2017) *Marxism and Psychoanalysis: In or against psychology?* London and New York: Routledge. [David Pavón Cuéllar, a Mexican Marxist and psychoanalytic writer, gives a detailed overview of the ways that different kinds of Marxism have been taken up an integrated into different kinds of psychoanalysis]

Sheehi, L. and Sheehi, S. (2021) *Psychoanalysis Under Occupation: Practicing Resistance in Palestine*. London and New York: Routledge. [Lara Sheehi and Stephen Sheehi, Lebanese activists, describe in detail the way that psychoanalysis works in conditions of Israeli colonial occupation in a book that stands with the oppressed, exemplifying what radical psychoanalysis could be]

Follow these ideas about radical psychoanalysis and take them forward. There are suggestions for further reading here https://fiimg.com/2021/11/19/radical-psychoanalysis-reading/ (or at this quicklink: https://bit.ly/3Fxcrf2).

Anti*Capitalist Resistance is committed to building a form of politics that works for liberation for all of the exploited and oppressed in this wretched world. We fight for the building of a world in which, as Marx put it, the free development of each is the condition for the free development of all. Read, think, act, join us.

WHAT IS A*CR

Anti*Capitalist Resistance is an organisation of revolutionary socialists. We believe red-green revolution is necessary to meet the compound crisis of humanity and the planet.

We are internationalists, ecosocialists, and anti-capitalist revolutionaries. We oppose imperialism, nationalism, and militarism, and all forms of discrimination, oppression, and bigotry. We support the self-organisation of women, Black people, disabled people, and LGBTQI+ people. We support all oppressed people fighting imperialism and forms of apartheid, and struggling for self-determination, including the people of Palestine.

We favour mass resistance to neoliberal capitalism. We work inside existing mass organisations, but we believe grassroots struggle to be the core of effective resistance, and that the emancipation of the working class and the oppressed will be the act of the working class and the oppressed ourselves.

We reject forms of left organisation that focus exclusively on electoralism and social-democratic reforms. We also oppose top-down 'democratic-centralist' models. We favour a pluralist organization that can learn from struggles at home and across the world.

We aim to build a united organisation, rooted in the struggles of the working class and the oppressed, and committed to debate, initiative, and self-activity. We are for social transformation, based on mass participatory democracy.

info@anticapitalistresistance.org
www.anticapitalistresistance.org

ABOUT RESISTANCE BOOKS

Resistance Books is a radical publisher of internationalist, ecosocialist, and feminist books. We publish books in collaboration with the International Institute for Research and Education in Amsterdam (www.iire.org) and the Fourth International (www.fourth.international/en). For further information, including a full list of titles available and how to order them, go to the Resistance Books website.

info@resistancebooks.org
www.resistancebooks.org

www.ingramcontent.com/pod-product-compliance
Lightning Source LLC
LaVergne TN
LVHW011853060526
838200LV00054B/4310